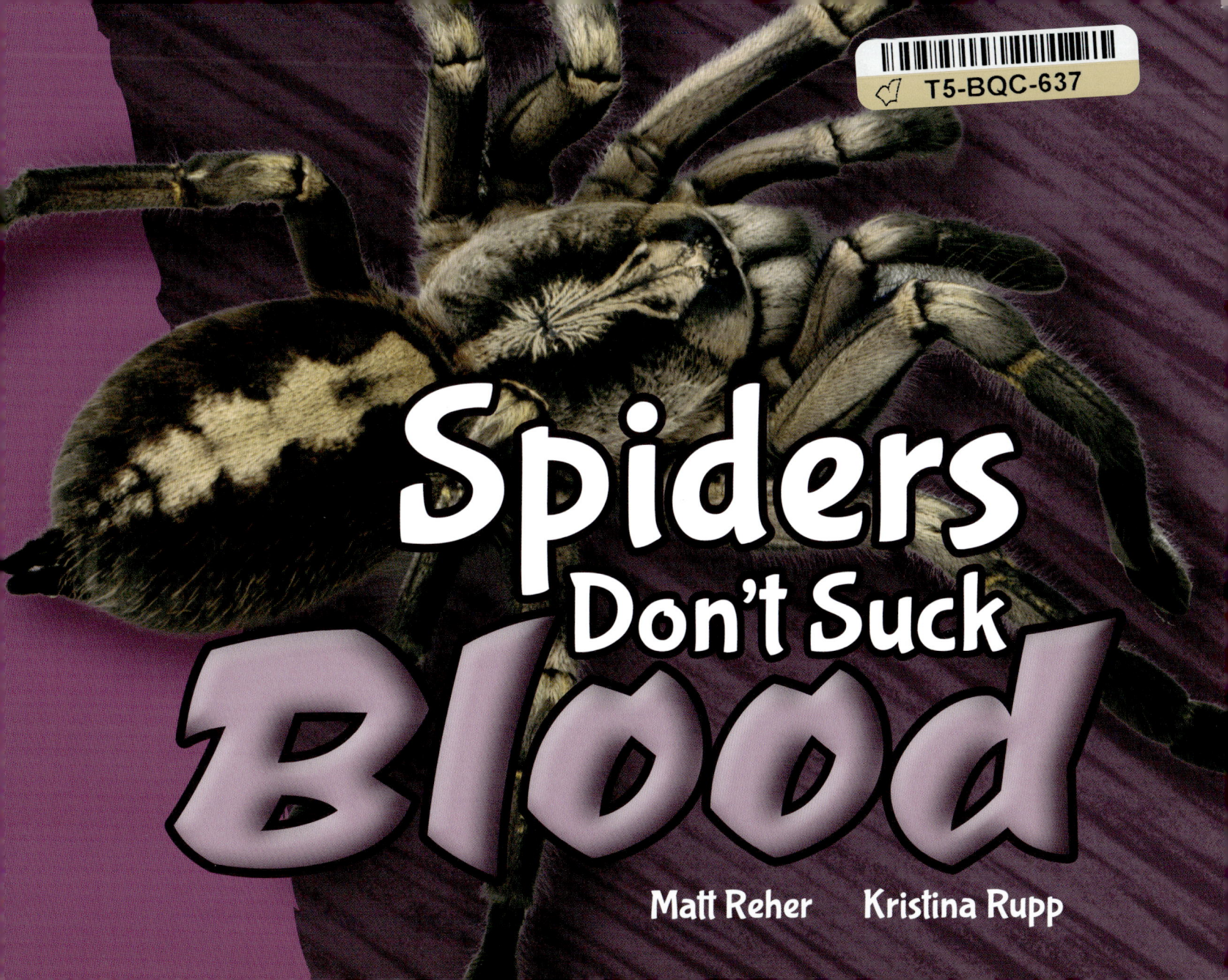

Spiders Don't Suck Blood

Matt Reher   Kristina Rupp

Spiders live all over the world.

Spiders are meat eaters. They eat bugs, frogs, birds, and other animals. The animals they eat are called their prey.

Yum!

Some people think spiders suck blood from their prey, but this isn't true.

They don't suck blood, but they can't bite and chew their food either. So, how do they eat?

All spiders have sharp mouth parts. They're made up of a base and a fang.

Spiders keep a liquid in their fangs called venom. They use the venom for catching and killing their prey.

venom

It's easy for the sharp fangs to go through the bug's hard shell.

Now, the spider can use its venom. The venom goes into the bug's body through the fangs.

The bug can't move.
Soon, it will die.

The spider starts grinding up the mushy bug meat with its mouth parts. The bug becomes bug soup.

The spider vomits, grinds up the bug, and sucks up the bug soup. It does this again and again until the soup is all gone.

Slurp!

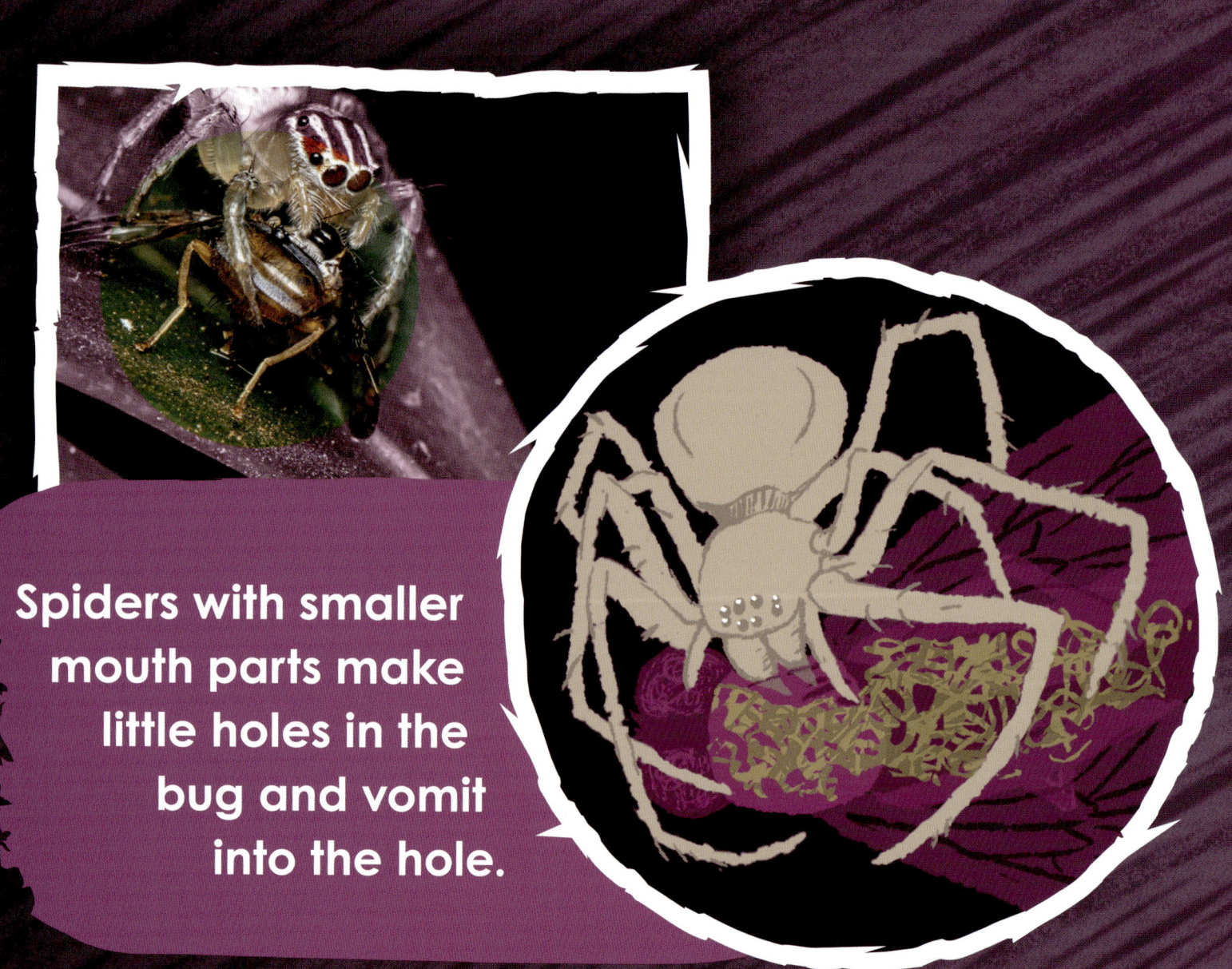

Spiders with smaller mouth parts make little holes in the bug and vomit into the hole.

The bug's insides become bug soup. The spider starts sucking up its meal through the holes.

Some spiders can eat very large prey, even if the prey is bigger than they are!

common house gecko
3 to 6 inches long

One of these spiders is called a banana spider.

Banana spiders build webs that can catch a flying bird!

These spiders have been known to eat snakes that are as long as this book!

Wait... WHAT?!?

Don't be scared. Spiders almost never bite people. Many spiders have fangs that are too short to hurt us. They think bug soup tastes better than people, anyway.

Meet the Banana Spider

male
actual size

female
actual size

Banana spiders have many names. People call them golden silk orb weavers, calico spiders, or giant wood spiders, too.

They live in warmer climates all over the world.

They spin webs with silk that's the color of gold. People have used the silk in fishing, clothing, and the medical field. It's said to be stronger than steel!

Male and female banana spiders look very different. The females are huge compared to the tiny males, but they work together to protect their eggs.

Two Kinds of Spider Venom

Neurotoxic
Venom that attacks the nerves of something bitten by a spider is called neurotoxic. In very rare cases, it can cause the death of a human by hurting the heart or lungs.

Necrotic
Venom that can break down and kill the tissue cells near a spider bite is called necrotic. In very rare cases, it can cause the death of a human by killing red blood cells.

black widow spider
neurotoxic venom

brown recluse spider
necrotic venom

Don't Be Scared!

The chance of being badly hurt by a spider is very, very slim. If bitten, it might hurt like a bee sting. The last thing a shy spider wants is to bite a person because no one likes getting squished!

Inflectional Ending Practice

Fill in the blank by matching the ending to the word.

-y   **-er**   **-ing**   **-ed**

1. A spider is a meat eat[__].

2. The web of a banana spider can catch a fly[__] bird.

3. Spider vomit makes bugs soft and mush[__].

4. The animals they eat are call[__] their prey.

Use the words you know to read new words!

all	get	will	put
ball	let	kill	push
call	bet	kills	mush
called	better	killing	mushy

Tricky Words

How many can you read?

body   build   gone